IMAGES
of America

FORT WASHINGTON AND UPPER DUBLIN

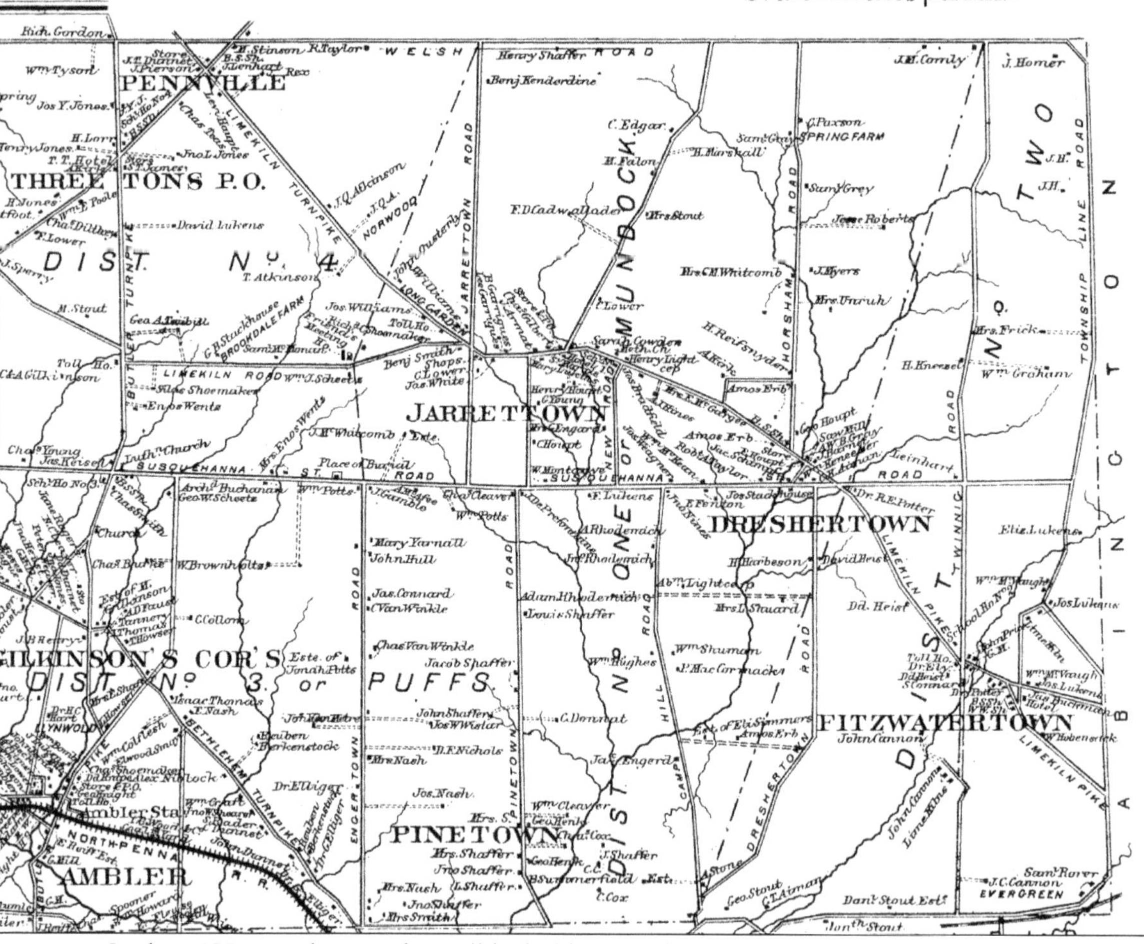

In this 1877 map, the township still looks like a patchwork quilt with many large farms. Some places on the map have been lost. Pennville, for example, has become known as Maple Glen due to the large expanse of maple trees throughout the area.

IMAGES
of America

FORT WASHINGTON AND UPPER DUBLIN

Historical Society of Fort Washington

ARCADIA
PUBLISHING

ISBN 978-1-5316-2043-1

Published by Arcadia Publishing
Charleston, South Carolina

Library of Congress Catalog Card Number: 2003116599

For all general information contact Arcadia Publishing at:
Telephone 843-853-2070
Fax 843-853-0044
E-mail sales@arcadiapublishing.com
For customer service and orders:
Toll-Free 1-888-313-2665

Visit us on the Internet at www.arcadiapublishing.com

The township of Upper Dublin, which dates from the beginning of the 19th century, included what is now the borough of Ambler. Early officials were known as supervisors of roads. Meetings were held in local public houses. In 1946, the township took over this house, at 1111 Bethlehem Pike, for its headquarters. The house was built as a private residence in 1886 by George and John Thomas, whose family owned significant acreage in the area as far back as the 1700s. In 1963, the township moved its headquarters to a new building on Loch Alsh Avenue, and the former building was bought by the Urbans for use as a funeral home.

Contents

Preface

Clifton House was built in 1801 on the site of the earlier Sandy Run Tavern. The tavern had been a stagecoach stop on the east side of the creek. Before the bridge was constructed over the Sandy Run Creek, people traveling from Philadelphia to Bethlehem experienced many problems crossing the waterway. The creek often flooded, making it necessary for the traveler to be provided with food and shelter while waiting for the water to recede.

Henry Daub built the stone tavern in 1801. The building saw many owners from that time until it reached its heyday under the guidance of owner George Herman in the last decade of the 19th century. Herman and his wife, Theresa Wentz, whose parents owned Hope Lodge, put in hot and cold running water and added a boat on the Sandy Run Creek for summer boarders. Articles in early editions of the *Ambler Gazette* indicate that lavish meals and dances were part of the vacationer's stay at Clifton House. The establishment continued to flourish until the advent of the automobile, which allowed people to travel beyond the confines of public transportation. Clifton House would no longer receive reservations for the season or even a month. The tavern experienced a rapid turnover of proprietors, and the building deteriorated badly. When the tavern was put up for sale in 1935, the Fairmount Park Commission purchased it with the idea of continuing Wissahickon Drive along the Sandy Run Creek, where it reached Fort Washington State Park. The plan was not put into effect, however, and the commission decided it would be better to tear down the decrepit structure.

In March 1935, a group of 33 local women met at the home of Mrs. Howard Buck to help preserve local history, homes, and buildings. The newly formed Historical Society of Fort Washington recognized the importance of saving the Clifton House. With the help of former Pennsylvania governor Gifford Pinchot, federal and state funds were acquired to purchase the building, and it was placed in the care of the historical society. Work Projects Administration (WPA) workers restored the building, and in 1937, the newly renovated Clifton House was leased to the historical society for the sum of $1 a year.

Today, almost 70 years later, Clifton House, at 473 Bethlehem Pike in Fort Washington, boasts rooms filled with furniture, artifacts, and books that give the public a look at this area's past. Rooms include the Victorian parlor, the meeting room, the Colonial kitchen, the Union schoolroom, and a reference library. The historical society meets on the third Tuesday of each month at 8:00 p.m., and the house is open for tours and research each Wednesday and on the first and third Sundays of the month from 2:00 to 4:00 p.m. Clifton House is closed the months of July and August. The telephone number of the historical society is 215-646-6065. Proceeds from the sale of this book will help to maintain Clifton House.

INTRODUCTION

Fort Washington takes its name from the defensive line set up by George Washington's soldiers after the Battle of Germantown. The soldiers positioned themselves along the hills running through both Upper Dublin and Whitemarsh townships. Many skirmishes took place in this area between the British and George Washington's troops in December 1777, before the British returned to Philadelphia. George Washington had his headquarters here at Emlen House from November 2 to December 11, 1777, before moving on to Valley Forge for the winter. The North Pennsylvania Railroad named the station Fort Washington where the railroad crosses Bethlehem Pike. The village of Fort Washington then grew up around the station.

In 1701, William Penn's surveyor, Thomas Holme, named Upper Dublin. This name described the 13-square-mile section of Montgomery County bounded roughly by today's Fitzwatertown Road, Welsh Road, Tennis Avenue, Morris Road, and Pennsylvania Avenue. The area was part of William Penn's land grant of 1681. English Quakers, Welshmen, and Germans began settling Upper Dublin as farmers shortly thereafter. They cleared the land and built rudimentary roads and homes to house their growing families. Thomas Fitzwater discovered limestone on his property and petitioned the Provincial Council in 1693 to build a road to get the lime from his kilns to Philadelphia, where it could be used in building mortar. Mills for grinding grain and cutting wood were built along the creeks. Blacksmith shops, wheelwright shops, and taverns developed soon thereafter. The sites for these services grew into early crossroads villages, which were named for early settlers and businessmen. Fitzwatertown, Dreshertown, Puff's Corner, Jarrettown, Gilkeson's Corner, and Engardtown are some examples. Other sites took their name from a business, such as Three Tuns, which was named for a tavern with three tuns, or kegs, on its sign. Taverns, or inns, were the centers of communication and socialization; the place where mail was left, political meetings were held, taxes were paid, official notices were posted, and voting was held. They also provided food and shelter for the horses and humans traveling the road to market or to the next village. Religious institutions and schools began to develop at these locations, as well.

The path of 18th-century development followed the roads that gave access to the area from Philadelphia and the surrounding settlements—Limekiln Pike (1693), Welsh Road (1712), Bethlehem Pike (1714), Jenkintown Road (1725), Butler Pike (1739 as Plymouth Road), Norristown Road (1751), and Susquehanna Street Road (1753). In the 19th century, turnpike companies were formed for Limekiln Pike, Butler Pike, and the Spring House-Chestnut Hill Turnpike to improve them through the collection of tolls.

The North Pennsylvania Railroad Company opened service through Fort Washington and the western edge of Upper Dublin in 1855. This led to the growth and separation of what became the borough of Ambler in 1888. The Trenton line was built across the township, and a station built at Dreshertown in 1888. These additions opened market opportunities to the area. Agricultural and nursery products could be sent more quickly to market on this line. Heavy industry developed along the railroads at Ambler, Edge Hill, Oreland, and Hoopeston. Housing was needed for the workers who followed. The Keasbey and Mattison Company built hundreds of homes for its workers in and around Ambler. The homes were constructed of local stone and ranged in design from stately houses with decorations like chess pieces, to simple row homes. Hoopes and Townsend Ironworks built a company town, Hoopeston, where today's office center is located.

The railroads also led to the building of grand country estates such as Camp Hill, Fairwold, and Quellehof. In addition, summer homes and resort hotels grew up near the stations, including Clifton House, today's headquarters for the Historical Society of Fort Washington. By 1890, the population in Upper Dublin had grown to 2,008, and by 1895, the Reading Company moved 18 trains per day to Philadelphia. The Fort Washington Fire Company was formed in January 1908. Additional churches and educational institutions were also established. The first horticultural school for women in the United States was founded in Upper Dublin in 1911 and later merged with Temple University. St. Mary's Orphanage took over 72 acres of the Mattison estate, Lindenwold, in 1936.

In spite of all this development, the primary business in Upper Dublin continued to be farming until well into the 20th century. Gradually, more homes were built near the railroad stations in Oreland and Fort Washington. This aided commuters who held jobs in Philadelphia. The greatest growth in these areas took place between 1921 and 1931. As more highways were built, especially the Pennsylvania Turnpike and state Route 309 Expressway, additional housing developments transformed Upper Dublin into a residential suburb of Philadelphia. Industries and other businesses developed in the Fort Washington Industrial Park beginning in the 1960s, and the area was gradually transformed into today's large office center.

Today, Fort Washington and Upper Dublin retain much of their historic past as they become first-class communities. This book provides readers with the opportunity to visit some places that no longer exist and to view the origins of continuing treasures. The communities have been presented in sequential order; from Fitzwatertown, the earliest established, to the most recently established, Fort Washington. We hope you will enjoy exploring these glimpses of the past.

—Robin Costa, President
Historical Society of Fort Washington

One

Fitzwatertown, Oreland, and North Hills

One of the earliest settlements in Upper Dublin was located along the Sandy Run Creek, an area rich in limestone and iron ore. Thomas Fitzwater built the first lime kilns along the creek. He petitioned the Provincial Council for a road from his kilns to Philadelphia in 1693. It was the first road built in Upper Dublin. Approximately 300 years after the first kiln was built, these visitors view the ruins of some similar kilns nearby.

The original gristmill at this site on Limekiln Pike was erected in the early 1700s by Thomas Fitzwater. He and his father, also Thomas, arrived with William Penn on the *Welcome* in 1682. In records from 1776, the younger Thomas's son John Fitzwater is shown as owning the mill and 300 acres, used as a picket outpost during the Whitemarsh Encampment. John Price operated the mill for many years, and at the time of this photograph, it belonged to Samuel Conard. Part of the building still stands.

In addition to the gristmill, Fitzwatertown had a hotel, store, wheelwright shop, blacksmith shop, schoolhouse, and about 12 homes. The school was located on Limekiln Pike at Twining Road, where a gas station and shopping center are now. Fitzwatertown had its own post office, beginning sometime before 1858. In 1850, the Limekiln Turnpike Company was formed to improve the road. Tollgates were erected, and tolls were collected until 1917. A tollhouse was on the west side of Limekiln Pike at Twining Road. The turnpike was gradually extended toward Jarrettown.

Charlotte Fitzwater, daughter of George and Elizabeth Fitzwater, was born in 1839 and married Dr. Robert E. Potter, who died in 1884. When this photograph was taken in 1896, the house belonged to her. It had at one time been the home of her grandfather John Fitzwater. It still stands on Lulu Country Club grounds facing Limekiln Pike, minus the porch and framed extension. Across the way was the old Fitzwater mill.

These visitors are paying their respects to the many Fitzwaters buried in the family cemetery on the Twining Road hill above the village in August 1896. The cemetery has two fieldstones marked with the initials T. F. and E. F., with the date 1771, as well as J. F., 1795. These appear to be memorials for Thomas, Elizabeth, and John Fitzwater, respectively. The cemetery is still in use.

Queen of Peace Catholic Church used this limestone quarry on Fitzwatertown Road as a grotto to honor the Blessed Mother before incorporating the area into the church parking lot. The church was founded in 1954 as an outgrowth of St. Luke, the Evangelist Church in Glenside. The quarry had been worked by the Lukens and Cannon families for the production of lime. The Lukens family settled on 200 acres in this part of the township early in the 1700s. Joseph Lukens set up limekilns along Fitzwatertown Road. Lime burning in this area continued into the 20th century.

This view of Julia Cannon's Rockdale farm buildings along Fitzwatertown Road was taken from Lincoln and G Avenues in Ardsley. The large barn on the left burned down. The carriage barn was converted to the first church for Queen of Peace parish. The house, believed to date from 1803, became the church rectory. Smoke from the limekilns, which operated at least until 1939, is visible in the background. Additional limekilns were located at Cedar Hollow, now part of Manufacturer's Golf and Country Club.

This *c.* 1890 photograph shows a group on the porch of the house at 1001 Fitzwatertown Road, between Susquehanna Street Road and Limekiln Pike. At that time, the house still belonged to the Lukens family, who can be traced back to the Lukens plantation in 1766. The last Lukens to live there sold the property to a nonrelative in 1909.

This view shows the Dannenberg barn, at 1001 Fitzwatertown Road, which is no longer standing. Built by Joseph Lukens, the farm was located a short distance from the limekilns. The kilns at this location continued to operate well into the 20th century.

Dr. Arthur Dannenberg and his wife, Marion, purchased this property in 1938 for a summer home. The farm on Fitzwatertown Road was about nine and a half acres and was named Dannybrook. This tract was a part of the 200-acre estate of William Lukens, partitioned in 1766. A portion of the house is believed to date from that period. Dannenberg, a Philadelphia pediatrician, and his family enjoyed spending summers at this location from 1938 until his death in 1990. He and his wife deeded the land to Upper Dublin Township for an arboretum in 1967. They continued to have use of the home throughout their lifetime. After severe deterioration, the property was subdivided and the house and two acres were sold and then restored as a private residence.

This home was built *c.* 1750 by George Emlen, a Quaker merchant from Philadelphia. It served as George Washington's headquarters during the Whitemarsh Encampment of November 2 through December 11, 1777. Caleb Emlen was the next owner until his death in 1816. In the early 19th century, the home had a series of owners including John Fitzwater. Charles T. Aiman owned it from 1857 to 1898. After his death, Sarah Van Renssalaer's daughter Frances Fell and her husband, Antelo Devereux, lived there and the property was known as Mistfield Farm. It was enlarged in 1929 by Frances and her second husband, Radcliffe Cheston. It was purchased with 90 acres in 1956 by the current owner, who enlarged it with a sunroom when rebuilding after a fire in 1974.

The home built for Howard and Mae Fell Henry between 1903 and 1904 was given the name Hawkswell; an addition was built in 1911. Mae, also a daughter of Sarah Van Renssalaer, lived there with her second husband, Gouvernor Cadwalader. The house was designed by architect Wilson Eyre Jr., who also established *House and Garden* magazine. It is located on Pennsylvania Avenue next to Emlen House. It currently serves as headquarters for the Copernicus and the Liberty Bell Foundations.

This frame house, at the corner of Orlando and Bala Avenues in Oreland, was built sometime before 1900, making it one of the oldest houses in the neighborhood. It no longer has the wraparound porch. The streets in this area were laid out by the Orlando Land & Improvement Company on land acquired from George Apel that had previously been part of the old Stout farm.

At the beginning of the 20th century, Herman Horn built a home and outbuildings along Pennsylvania Avenue at the corner of Apel Avenue. This area developed gradually after railroad service was established. Many of the homes were summer residences. Still standing, the Horn home has been renovated with professional offices on the ground floor and apartments above.

The homes built in the Upper Dublin part of Oreland during the 1920s were individual designs and not built as a housing development. They typically had three bedrooms with one bath, a full basement, and a one-car garage. Many of the residents used the railroad to commute to Philadelphia. This house on Wischman Avenue has been expanded like many others in this popular neighborhood.

These children are on the playground of the East Oreland School, next to the 1940s addition. The school was originally opened in 1909 and closed in 1965, when Sandy Run Elementary School opened. The building was then used for special education and administration. The two classrooms behind the children served as the Upper Dublin Public Library from 1966 until 1977, when the library moved to the former Sandy Run Elementary School. The building is now the East Oreland Program Intergenerational (EPI) Center.

Antioch Baptist Church began with informal meetings and Sunday School in the home of Birdella Tolson. A small church was erected in 1906 on Chelsea Avenue. A charter was obtained in 1908. A second church building was erected in 1915 and demolished in 1931, when this church was built. The Reverend Joseph Jackson served as pastor for 26 years—from April 1939 until his death in December 1965.

The Missionary Circle of Antioch Baptist Church supported activities both nearby and abroad. Assembled in this 1943 photograph are, from left to right, the following: (first row) Louise James, Ella Wilson, Julia Gaskins, Ella Phillips, and Lena Brown; (second row) Evelyn Cottom, Sina Wilson, Odessa Johnson, Bertha Wallace, Laura Holmes, and Sue Armstead; (third row) the Reverend Joseph W. Jackson.

The North Glenside School, at 212 Girard Avenue in North Hills, was built in 1926 and served children in grades one through eight. Later, kindergarten was added and the seventh and eighth grades were moved to Upper Dublin Junior High School. In addition to regular classrooms, the school had a home economics and a manual arts room in the basement. Evelyn Wright served as teacher and then principal at the school from its opening until it closed in 1965. The building is now the North Hills Community Center and has a branch of the Upper Dublin Public Library.

Members of the sixth-grade class in 1954 are celebrating their graduation. In the front row are, from left to right, Morgan Brown, Gloria Holmes, William Richardson, and Myrna Pinkett.

Two

DRESHERTOWN

Dreshertown, known as Dresher today, developed around a sawmill and gristmill built by John Kirk before 1750. George Dresher bought the mill *c.* 1780, and the family owned it for 54 years. Sometime during that period, the village became known as Dreshertown. Dresher also served as an Upper Dublin supervisor in 1788 and 1792. He died in 1803 and is buried in the family cemetery on Dreshertown Road.

The Dresher family came from Silesia, Germany, and arrived in Philadelphia with a group of Schwenkfelders in 1734. Grandson George Dresher established himself as a businessman. Like many settlers at that time, the Dreshers established a small burial ground close to their residence. The cemetery is located on Dreshertown Road just east of Limekiln Pike. The earliest gravestone is marked 1803. Many descendants of the Dresher family are buried here.

Early farmhouses dot the Upper Dublin landscape. This property still stands at the corner of Kirk Lane and Dreshertown Road. An 1877 land map shows a house and barn at this location that was owned by a person named Reifsnyder. The barn no longer stands but was still shown in photographs as late as 1972.

Charles Paxson moved from Cheltenham in 1826 to a farm purchased by his father, Joshua, on Dreshertown Road. The farm was part of the Spencer property, received as a grant from William Penn. Paxson's great-grandson, the current owner, is a member of the Upper Dublin Association of Montgomery County for the Recovery of Stolen Horses, Detection of Horse Thieves and Obtaining Other Stolen Property. Charles Paxson, was a charter member of this group, which was founded in 1828.

This salt cellar was located near the intersection of Susquehanna Road and Limekiln Pike. Salt cellar construction is characterized by its uneven roofline, which is longer on the back of the building. It was used to store salt, a precious commodity before the advent of refrigeration. A bushel of salt cost 25 shillings in 1777. The salt was used primarily for preservation of food but was also required for livestock. Some of these salt cellars were later converted into small houses.

The Dreshertown post office was established in 1832 and was once located at the corner of Dreshertown Road and Limekiln Pike. Mail was not received on a daily basis and was picked up from the post office, which also contained a small general store. Township elections were held here from 1840 to 1856. Soon thereafter, the post office closed and mail service moved to Jarrettown. This photograph shows extensive modernization before the building was demolished.

A county map of 1871 shows this property as belonging to a J. Schimpf. By the early 20th century, ownership had transferred to J. McMullin. The house is located at the corner of Susquehanna Road and Peg Street. After many years and several renovations, the last being in the mid-1970s, the house was converted it into its present configuration as a delicatessen and pizzeria.

Train service came to Upper Dublin in 1855, with the Trenton cutoff added in 1888. This railroad bridge carries the Trenton line over Camp Hill Road and is about one and a half miles west of the Camp Hill Station near the spot where the famous train wreck of 1856 occurred. The collision was so fierce that the wooden carriages went up in flames. More than 100 people were severely injured, and more than 60 people were killed. Among the rescuers was Mary Ambler, after whom the town of Ambler was named.

The Pennsylvania Railroad was built through the area in 1888 and had a station at Dreshertown close to where Susquehanna Road and Limekiln Pike cross. It handled both passengers and freight, considerably shortening the trip to Philadelphia or Trenton. By 1895, there were 18 trains to Philadelphia each day. In May 1902, the railroad company announced that all milk and passenger trains would be discontinued. After a successful petition by local residents, the company agreed to continue with the trains. Although freight trains still run, passenger service has been discontinued and the station torn down.

Francis Houpt (Haupt) ran a general store in the triangle of Peg Street, Susquehanna Road, and Limekiln Pike from sometime before 1871 to *c.* 1916. This section was the center of the village where most of the businesses were located. In the Houpt store, customers could buy dry goods, groceries, hardware, notions, drugs, and paints. After the first Dreshertown post office had closed, it was reestablished in 1885 in the Houpt store, and at this time, Francis Houpt was appointed postmaster. It is unclear what happened to the store after 1916. The Houpt family name appears in Upper Dublin at least as far back as the middle of the 18th century.

Shown here are loungers in front of the Houpt store *c.* 1905. The general store was as much a social center as it was a commercial enterprise. People came not only to do their shopping but also to hang around, read the paper, shoot the breeze, or merely wile away some time. As can be seen in the photograph, even the young joined their elders in this activity or lack thereof.

The McCormick Brothers Wagon Builders and Blacksmith Shop, above, built wagons from 1900 to 1920. With the advent of motor vehicles, the business and demand for wagons fell off. The backyard of a wheelwright and blacksmith shop appears in the lower right corner of the picture below. The men are probably waiting for their horses to be shod or their wagons to be repaired. The properties were part of the Dresher Triangle, where Susquehanna Road and Limekiln Pike cross.

Peg Street is shown above in a view looking west toward Susquehanna Road and the Meehan Nursery. The Meehan family started the nursery business in Dresher in 1912 and became very successful. Several other nurseries flourished along Susquehanna Road and Limekiln Pike. Looking north, the view below shows Limekiln Pike with the Houpt store, a barn, and a wagon shed on the left. Early photographs of Limekiln Pike indicate that the road was merely a "cart way," but as population grew and traveling increased, demands for a proper open road arose. Limekiln Pike was built in stages from village to village. In the Dresher area, it was a toll road until 1917, with a tollhouse at each end of the village.

The history of the Dresher Inn is rather sketchy. This photograph shows the residence of A. D. Barnett (Burnett), the owner of a coal company from 1902 to 1927. Barnett also operated a nursery, and sometime in the 1930s, he bought more land from the nearby T. Meehan & Sons Nursery when they sold their business and divided their property. Half of the land became known as the Burnett & Lane Nursery, and the other half was acquired by Frederick Schmidt. Just when the property was converted to a restaurant is not clear. However, it served in this capacity until the 1970s. Today, the building stands unoccupied.

This old blacksmith shop stood at the northeast corner of Dreshertown Road and Limekiln Pike. Records show that it was still in operation in the early 20th century, although little else is known. It served the many farmers and residents in the Dresher area. There are at least 11 signs advertising celluloid starch on the building. It is not clear whether these serve as advertisements or building repair.

This view looks north from the Trenton cutoff of the Pennsylvania Railroad. Susquehanna Road is on the left with the Pine Run Creek meandering toward Dresher. The Meehan Nursery is on the left, the Houpt store in the center, and the Barnett's barn on the right.

Susquehanna Road was laid out on parchment by surveyor Thomas Holmes in 1683 at William Penn's direction. It was the reference point for measuring early land grants. The road itself was not built until c. 1753. In this picture, it is still shown as a "cart way." Its lovely rural setting was typical of the early 1900s.

The Francis Shrope residence stood on the current site of the Burn Brae Fire Station, at the corner of Susquehanna and Twining Roads. Part of the property was a nursery extending north to the railroad track, and the other half was a quarry. The Shropes moved to Dresher in 1908 and lived here until 1948. The property is now part of the Twining Valley Golf and Fitness Club.

In the early 1920s, nursing homes started to appear in Upper Dublin because of its "country air." The Jewish Convalescents Home was built by the Federation of Jewish Charities in June 1929. It stood on Welsh Road east of Dreshertown Road where the Prudential Office Buildings are now located. It contained all the facilities necessary to restore health, including therapeutic and examination rooms, a gymnasium, and a playground.

The Clime (Clive) Farm was built in 1789 for the Clime family. In 1921, Henry and Maria Nelson bought 37 acres, part of which was a nursery. The place was primarily a chicken farm, but the Nelsons also owned pigs, cows, and workhorses, and they grew vegetables for their huckster route in Philadelphia. Farmed until the early 1950s, the property remained in the family until *c.* 2000, when a group of developers bought it.

This picture shows people enjoying a Sunday drive along Susquehanna Road in a 1917 Model T Ford. By 1917, the price of the Model T Ford touring car had fallen below $500. This allowed the average middle-class person to afford one. By 1923, the price had dropped to $290, at which time the working family could afford one. It is interesting to note that in 1917 there were 325,123 motor vehicles registered in Pennsylvania. By 1922, that number had climbed to 689,589.

In 1935, Frederick Schmidt, a German immigrant, purchased this house located in the Dresher Triangle, half of the Lane Nursery, and some acreage of the Meehan Nursery. The small building next to the residence was the business office. At the time, 16 houses and businesses were located in the Dresher Triangle. The *c.* 1940 photograph, above, was taken from across Limekiln Pike. The other photograph shows Schmidt's wife, Martha, sitting on the bumper of their 1937 Plymouth, parked next to the office. The family still operates a nursery on Limekiln Pike.

Taken *c.* 1970, this aerial view of Dresher shows two of the earliest buildings at the northeast end of the Industrial Park, as it was then called. The whole area of the Fort Washington Industrial Park along this stretch of Susquehanna Road is now fully developed, and the Industrial Park has been transformed into the Fort Washington Business and Office Center. The road from the center left to the upper right is Susquehanna Road. The Clime Farm is the first house north of the Dresher Triangle on Susquehanna Road. Note the farmland, and at the right center, a nursery. The lower road is Limekiln Pike.

Three

JARRETTOWN

The Jarret family came from Scotland and settled in the Upper Dublin area in the early 18th century. Members of a large farming family, the Jarrets owned several properties in Upper Dublin. This house was built in 1734 near the corner of Dillon and Welsh Roads. It is believed that this house is one of the first houses to have been built in this part of Upper Dublin and that Jarrettown is named after this family.

The Donat property was located on Dillon Road where Temple Sinai is today. The Donat family owned the land from 1892 until sometime in the mid-20th century. A portion of the house was built in the late 18th century, according to documentation found in the walls in 1932.

This old building, showing the ravage of years of neglect, stood at the south corner of Dillon Road and Limekiln Pike. The property was owned by the Lowers (Lauers), who were wagon builders. In Charles Donat's recollection, this corner was quite the hub of commercial activity in the latter half of the 19th century, serving the farming community, which was very extensive at that time. The barn no longer exists, and the site is part of Temple Sinai.

The Jarrettown Hotel is located on Limekiln Pike in Jarrettown. It was built by Henry Houpt (Haupt) in 1847 on three acres of land purchased in 1759 by Samuel Houpt, Henry's grandfather. The property had passed out of the hands of the Houpt family five years before the hotel was built. Henry Houpt owned the business for 22 years and then sold it to Nathan Marples in 1865. Upon the death of Marples, the hotel was inherited by his wife, Sarah. Although Sarah Marples and her heirs owned the hotel until 1902, they did not operate the business; Charles Palmer served as innkeeper of the renamed Palmer Hotel. It is presumed because of the name change that Palmer leased the premises rather than served as an employee. During his tenure, the hotel was slightly damaged by the tornado of 1896. Irvin Rotzell purchased the hotel for $12,000 in 1902, the same year telephones were installed. In 1939, he sold the hotel to John and Clara Schmitt, in whose family it remained until 1997. Today, the Jarrettown Hotel operates as a restaurant.

This barn, or "large shed," located on Limekiln Pike next to the Palmer Hotel (Jarrettown Hotel), was severely damaged in the tornado of 1896. Accounts differ, as is so often the case. However, all agree that a wall collapsed killing two men and some horses—either two or five. The men who died were Winfield Ensley (Emelie) of Philadelphia and Alfred Moffit (Moffat), a hostler employed at the hotel. Injured were John Hamill and his wife, who had just driven in; John Betts, a huckster; and Fred Spencer (Spence), age 13. The people had sought refuge in the building because the walls were made of stone. A group of 21 men came from Ambler to assist in caring for the injured and to seek bodies still buried in the rubble.

The Jarrettown post office and store was established in the village in 1866 on Limekiln Pike. An 1893 map shows the location to be on the north corner of Limekiln Pike and what was then Horsham Road (Jarrettown Road). This photograph shows the post office at 1457 Limekiln Pike, previously a carriage-painting shop. After the post office closed on November 26, 1971, and moved to another location, William Rodemich bought this building and built the present house around it.

The original one- or two-room Jarrettown School was built *c.* 1805 at Limekiln Pike and Mundock Road on land donated by Henry Houpt. Accounts vary as to what happened to the original building. One account says that it was "heavily damaged in the 1896 tornado and rebuilt." However, this photograph of the school, taken soon after the tornado (August 3, 1896), shows a structure that had already been enlarged.

The Jarrettown Public School No. 1 was rebuilt after the 1896 tornado. It was one of four public schools in the villages of Upper Dublin. Although Schools No. 2 and No. 3 are no longer in existence, School No. 4 can still be seen at the corner of Butler Pike and Norristown Road. The Jarrettown School was closed in 1926. Significantly modified, the building still stands and is a preschool.

The sign in front of the Jarrettown School at Limekiln Pike and Mundock Road reads, "Upper Dublin Public School, No. 1, Rebuilt in 1896," having been damaged by a tornado earlier that year. The present Jarrettown Elementary School opened in 1955 across Limekiln Pike.

Members of the class of 1917 and their schoolmaster pose for a photograph outside the Jarrettown School. Anna Nelson is seated second from the left in the second row. The school provided education through the eighth grade, offering subjects such as Latin, algebra, geography, civil government, and ancient history, preparing students to go to high school in any of the surrounding townships. Upper Dublin's first high school class graduated in 1955.

The busing of school students started in Upper Dublin in 1921, according to some records. Jarrettown resident Raymond Smith, pictured at the wheel of a Dodge Brothers model, was hired as bus driver and mechanic at that time, and the first school bus purchased was a Packard. After their school was closed in 1926, students from Jarrettown were bused to Fort Washington Elementary School, on Madison Avenue. This photograph was taken c. 1927. A third bus was purchased in 1945 for the school district.

The Jarrettown Methodist Episcopal Church was established in March 1865 at the Philadelphia Annual Conference of the Methodist Episcopal Church. Previous religious meetings were held in private homes, beginning in 1844. The first sermon was preached in the Mundock School, later known as Jarrettown Public School. A church school started at this time and very quickly flourished, having an average attendance of 50 pupils. The teachers were all young local people, whose names were Houpt, Donat, and Lower, and were not members of the newly organized church. By October 1865, a building committee was appointed to secure a suitable site for the church. In the spring of 1866, a one-acre lot was purchased for $200 from Abram Kirk, and the building was erected at the current location. An additional third of an acre was acquired a year later, and on September 16, 1866, the church building was dedicated. This picture is of the rebuilt church, which was dedicated on February 14, 1897. In 1966, a new sanctuary was added to this still active church.

Dedicated on September 16, 1866, the original Jarrettown Methodist Episcopal Church was almost an exact copy of the Milestown Church (Oak Lane United Methodist Church)—a one-story building with two doors in the front opening directly into the sanctuary, two aisles from the front doors leading to the pulpit, and the altar rising at the far end of the room. Church members are shown inspecting the building after it was partially destroyed by the 1896 tornado.

The original edifice was considered to be a fine example of a country church. The interior was arranged in the usual design of that time. The pews had a partition in the center, probably to separate the ladies from the men. A heavy cornice of plaster of Paris extended around the room, and an ornate centerpiece adorned the ceiling.

This house was constructed in 1878, as evidenced by the year placed in red slate tiles on the roof facing Limekiln Pike. The building at one time was the home of the Independent Order of Odd Fellows No. 458, which held its meetings on the third floor. The order was founded on November 17, 1851.

Located on Mundock Road, this farmhouse dates back to 1742 and has seen many alterations and modernizations. A stone-banked barn is all that remains of the original farmstead. The interior of the barn has been redesigned and converted into living quarters, maintaining its outside features. Once a working farm, the property is now surrounded by new houses. The place has had several owners besides the current ones, who purchased it in 1930.

The photograph above shows the Seiriano-Winslow property on the east side of Limekiln Pike. It was built in 1888 and purchased by Mrs. Seiriano, Mrs. Winslow's mother, in 1920. The Winslow family still lives here. An early map of 1871 shows that the property was once owned by Charles Gilbert and had a building on it. The photograph below, taken from the Winslow house during the 1976 bicentennial celebration, shows Limekiln Pike, with the Jarrettown Hotel and the horse-drawn wagons reenacting the evacuation of the Liberty Bell from Philadelphia to Allentown.

Four

THREE TUNS AND MAPLE GLEN

The village of Three Tuns developed at the crossroads of today's Butler Pike and Norristown Road. A tavern built c. 1748 on land owned by Jacob Timanus gave the location its name. Its sign showed three wine casks, or tuns. In 1803, John Collom built his house at this location and received a license to operate the inn shortly thereafter.

Three Tuns Inn was an important location for Upper Dubliners. School teacher interviews, Unionist meetings, and court sessions were all held there. In February 1828, the Association for the Recovery of Stolen Horses, Detention of Horse Thieves and Obtaining Other Stolen Property had its first meeting in the inn. A sizable wing was added to the west corner of the old house after B. W. Zeetz, former proprietor of the Fortside Inn, purchased it in 1906. The inn served as a place of food, fodder, and rest for 145 years until it burned down on March 4, 1948.

The original schoolhouse at Three Tuns, Upper Dublin School No. 4, was a frame structure approximately 16 feet square. Its schoolmaster was Amos Lewis. That building was replaced in 1860 by this stone structure. Close to the school was a blacksmith shop operated by Jake Lenhart.

The Three Tuns Schoolhouse was extensively remodeled in 1913. After it closed in 1923, students were transported to the Fort Washington Elementary School. The School District sold the property in 1925. Since then, it has been a private residence.

In 1833, Clement Jones built Three Tuns Store across from the Three Tuns Inn, at the intersection of Butler Pike and Norristown Road. The store housed the Union Library of Upper Dublin until 1888. Founded in 1834, the library circulated the personal books of the founders and later moved to the new Borough of Ambler. A post office was established at the store in 1858. The store was demolished by Wilmer Atkinson to build his home, North View, in the 1880s.

Wilmer Atkinson built North View on Butler Pike in 1887. He named the farm Quinby for his mother's family. It was a model farm for the publisher, owner, and founder of the *Farm Journal* magazine. Atkinson financed the building of Butler Pike. Fruit from his farm was a bonus for those who used the turnpike. The home withstood an attempt by the man who purchased the property from Atkinson to turn it into a roadhouse during Prohibition.

This original plaster-over-stone farmhouse, on Fort Washington Avenue at Limekiln Pike, was built in 1793 with additions in 1849 and the early 1900s. The property was originally purchased by a Quaker named William Atkinson, who arrived from England as a child in 1699. His father, who did not survive the voyage, had a land grant in Bucks County from William Penn. William Atkinson was raised there by Quakers and moved to this location as an adult. He willed the property to his granddaughter, who erected this house and the barn and donated part of the land to the Friends Meeting for a meetinghouse. The farm was later known as Cherry Lane Farm. In 1998, the property was purchased from the Edwards family by the Upper Dublin School District, and the house and barn were converted for use as administrative offices.

The barn and tenant house for the Atkinson farm were built by Phoebe Shoemaker. During the 1850s, when the Fugitive Slave law was enacted, Thomas and Hannah Atkinson and their neighbors operated a branch of the Underground Railroad. They gave shelter to runaway slaves, who were brought to the farm and concealed overnight before being transported to Bucks County.

The Upper Dublin Friends Meeting House, at the corner of Fort Washington Avenue and Meetinghouse Road, was built in 1814 on land donated by Phoebe Shoemaker. The building has many of its original characteristics, such as the handblown glass panes in its windows. A small addition was recently added to the original structure. The Religious Society of Friends still holds weekly worship in the building. Adjoining the meetinghouse is the graveyard where many early residents of Upper Dublin are buried.

J. H. Ringe Jr. bought this property in 1877 from Henry Jones and rebuilt the mansion. The farm was once known as Waldheim Farm. Situated in a 20th-century neighborhood, this well-preserved 1850s building still stands at 1707 Penns Lane, in the Three Tuns area of Upper Dublin.

Wilmer Atkinson designed this building for a library and post office after tearing down the Three Tuns Store, which had earlier housed these services. The building stood on the edge of Atkinson's property along Butler Pike. When Atkinson left Three Tuns in 1915, the post office closed and the books were transferred to the *Farm Journal* office for use by its employees. Although the building has been demolished, the entrance steps are still visible from Butler Pike.

This Greek Revival home still stands at 1815 Butler Pike. Built in 1846, Hidenach Farm was built by physician Joshua Jones. Jones, the son of a doctor, graduated from the University of Pennsylvania in 1830. Elected to the state senate in 1852, he also served as a commissioner for the centennial celebration of 1876.

This home stood at 1800 Butler Pike, where Cedar Hedge Farm was originally located. From 1986 to 2003, when it was demolished for new construction, the building served as a healthcare facility called the Elizabeth Home.

This impressive stone structure stands on part of the original Wilmer Atkinson property at 1636 Butler Pike. Its Colonial Revival architecture indicates it was built *c.* 1900. In 1947, the property became home to the first accredited preschool and kindergarten in Pennsylvania, Twin Spring Farm Day School and Camp. The Three Tuns area contained many large homes, such as this one, that remain standing today.

This is a view of the entrance to the Pennsylvania School of Horticulture for Women as it appeared in the early 1900s. The campus was a farm of 71 acres when Jane Bowne Haines purchased it in 1910. She had visited several colleges of gardening in England and recognized a need for horticulture instruction in American education. In 1958, the school merged with Ambler Junior College of Temple University and opened the program to men. In 1961, it became the Ambler Campus of Temple University.

Students observe a lesson in tree pruning—one of the many subjects taught at the Pennsylvania School of Horticulture for Women, which, when it opened in 1911, was the only school of its type in the United States. Classes began on February 11, 1911, with a grand total of five students. Today, Temple University at Ambler has a population of more than 4,700 students. It added bachelor degree programs in landscape architecture and horticulture in 1987.

These students made up the 1916 graduating class of the Pennsylvania School of Horticulture for Women. Louise Carter Bush-Brown, who was director from 1924 to 1952, is at the left. Under her leadership, the school increased its enrollment and initiated degree programs. She also attracted women from diverse cultures such as Japan, Australia, and West Germany. Her husband, James Bush-Brown, who served on the faculty in the 1920s and 1930s, designed the nationally acclaimed formal gardens. A dormitory was built in 1929 and a library in 1951.

Temple University at Ambler welcomed thousands of visitors each year to a wide variety of entertainment events from Ella Fitzgerald to Bill Cosby to the Electric Light Orchestra. Temple University Music Festival was held during the summer from 1968 to 1980.

Five

Gilkey's Corner and the Ambler Area

The house at 306 Stout Road is considered to be one of the oldest in Upper Dublin. It was built just off the Province Road (Butler Pike) for tax collector Thomas Seddon in 1702. For many years it was associated with the Stout family. A two-story addition was built in the 1860s.

Gilkey's Corner, the intersection of Bethlehem Pike and Butler Pike, was named for Andrew Gilkeson, who operated a tavern there from at least 1778 until his death in 1814. By 1803, he had replaced the small tavern with a larger stone building to accommodate the increasing number of travelers using the Great Road to transport goods from Lehigh County to Philadelphia. Official business, such as paying taxes and voting, was also conducted there. An Upper Dublin post office was added in 1818. After Gilkeson's death, sons James and Samuel Gilkeson continued to operate the tavern and store until Samuel's death in 1847. In 1884, Theodore Bean, in his history of Montgomery County, described Gilkey's corner as having the "store, 6 or 7 houses and the extensive steam tannery of Alvin D. Faust."

In 1871, David Dunnet operated the Gilkey's Corner store, at Butler and Bethlehem Pikes. His business listing for that year showed him dealing in dry goods, groceries, hardware, drugs, paints, oils, boots, and shoes. The area became known as Rose Valley in the 1880s. Robert McIlroy leased the general store from the early 1900s until 1921. In 1921, John Martin added a tearoom and operated the store until he sold it to Joseph Stout in 1924. George W. Porter purchased the store from Stout in 1929. He operated it as a general store until 1950. Then, he sold it to Charles Sandilos, who installed a grill, enlarged the sandwich menu, and changed the name to Rose Valley Delicatessen. Since 1951, it has been Costa's Delicatessen.

This photograph shows the actual quarry where the stone was harvested for the Mattison house (now St. Mary's), Trinity Memorial Church, and the many homes that were constructed for the Keasbey and Mattison workers. The quarry was located at the corner of Farm Lane and Highland Avenue.

This 1953 aerial view of the intersection formerly known as Gilkey's Corner shows the old Gilkeson store, now Costa's Delicatessen, in the upper right. Across the street are, from right to left, Mullin Motors, Catanzaro's store and apartments, a residence, and Ambler Church of the Brethren. In the center, surrounded by parking, is the Howard Johnson's Restaurant. Across Bethlehem Pike and slightly to the north is the location of the former Faust Tannery.

The congregation of the Upper Dublin German Baptist Church assembled along the Butler Pike roadway for this 1922 photograph. This 28- by 36-foot meetinghouse was built at Butler Pike and Hagues Mill Road on land donated by John Reiff in 1840. It was also known as the Dunkard Church. At the right of the photograph, behind the tree, are the sheds for horses and carriages. Some worshipers rode the trolley on Bethlehem Pike to Butler Pike and then walked the half-mile to the church. The congregation built a new church in the borough of Ambler that was dedicated in 1923. This building no longer stands in Upper Dublin, but the church still maintains its graveyard on the property. Today, the church is known as Ambler Church of the Brethren.

This building of the Upper Dublin Evangelical Lutheran Church was built in 1857. It was remodeled and enlarged in 1899 on property donated by Valentin Puff in the 1750s. This corner of Butler Pike and Susquehanna Road was known as Puff's Corner. Diagonally across from the church was Puff's School. A log building at this site housed the original church between 1753 and 1810. During the Revolutionary War, the church was used as a hospital for American soldiers. Several patriots who died in the battle of Germantown are buried in its cemetery. John B. Sterigere, a dominant political leader in Montgomery County, was instrumental in reorganizing the congregation in 1852 and getting the church built. He is buried in the adjoining graveyard. Replaced by a new building across Susquehanna Road, this building was torn down in 1974.

James Morris built this gristmill in 1777 with lumber left behind by the Virginia troops who had encamped there. In 1798, Adam Wertsner bought the mill, located on Morris Road near Butler Pike. He added a cider mill, which became a prosperous business. After he died, his son and grandson operated the mill. It was demolished in 1887.

This barn was designed by well-known architect Horace Trumbauer for Charles W Bergner as part of his 93-acre Abendruh (German for "evening rest") estate. It was built with stone from the Farm Lane quarry in 1891. Sen. Edwin H. Vare purchased the estate from Bergner. The Wissahickon Valley Watershed Association now owns the property and uses it as a nature museum and offices.

In 1882, Dr. Richard V. Mattison and his partner, Henry G. Keasbey, moved their chemical works to Ambler to manufacture quinine and magnesia. The photograph shows the Mattison home, Lindenwold, before Milton Bean remodeled it in 1912 to resemble a Scottish castle. Although Mattison is known as the person responsible for building much of Ambler, his home actually is in Upper Dublin Township.

In 1912, R. V. Mattison encased his Victorian home in stone. Lansdale architect Milton Bean transformed the house into a Scottish castle. Compare the castle with the original house and notice the outlines are very similar. Mattison sold the property to the Sisters of the Holy Family of Nazareth in 1936. Since then, it has been used as a home for children.

Designed by Milton Bean, most of the entrance gates to Lindenwold stand today. The stonework above this entrance gate on Lindenwold Avenue is no longer there. The name Lindenwold is chiseled into the stone of some gates, indicating that that part is original. Ironwork now found on the Lindenwold Avenue gate indicates later work (1936), since it bears the name St. Mary's. Mattison brought workers from Italy to work in his factory. It is interesting to note that he did not bring artisans from Europe to work on his mansion. The ironwork and later changes were most likely done by local craftsmen.

The Mattison estate included a number of small structures, among them this stone gazebo. People who entered the estate from Lindenwold Avenue had to cross this bridge and pass the gazebo on their way to the main house. The stonework matches the work done on the mansion when Milton Bean created the castle in 1912.

In true Victorian fashion, the estate contained a six-acre lake, Loch Linden, stocked for fishing. A fountain with 62 jets purified the water and added to the adornment of the estate. Some of the lake does not exist today, but the placement of outbuildings gives visitors an indication of its former location.

R. V. Mattison built these homes on Lindenwold Terrace for the highest executives of the Keasbey and Mattison Company. The homes survive and are largely unchanged today. The block was designed as a mirror image of itself. The two end houses are of the same design as are the two next to the end houses, and so forth.

R. V. Mattison built Trinity Memorial Church in 1901 as a memorial to his daughter, Esther Victoria, who died in 1887 at age four. The stone was most likely from the nearby Farm Lane quarry. The edifice burned to the ground in June 1986. Later rebuilt, it still stands today, along with the rectory and the homes of company executives on Trinity Place.

This row of twin homes along Ambler Road was occupied by employees of Keasbey and Mattison. The final rows of homes, which R. V. Mattison had built on Renfrew and Randolph Avenues, were designed by architect John Bothwell. The employees rented the homes from Mattison.

This store, at the corner of Bannockburn Avenue and Church Street, was one of the buildings constructed by Mattison to serve his employees. In 1921, Fred S. Arnold became the first to occupy it, before establishing his business in Fort Washington. Frank Wright Sr. bought the store in 1923. The Wright family maintained a grocery store and delicatessen there until 1960.

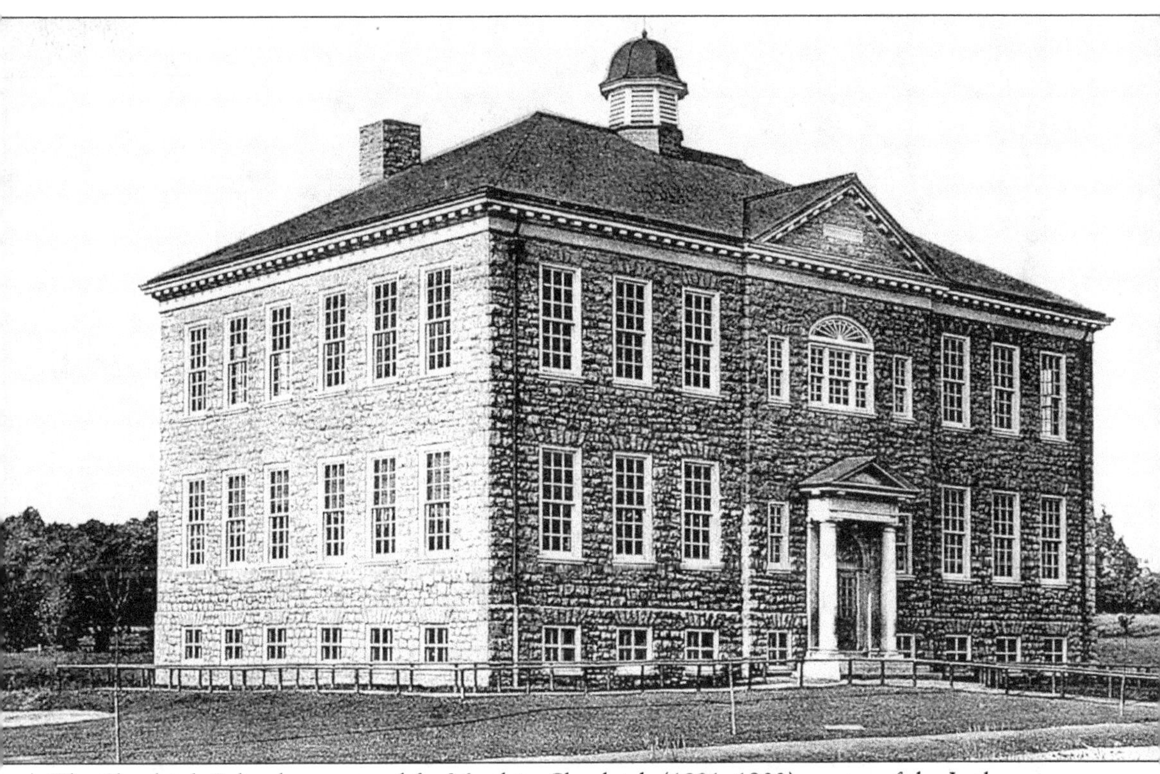

The Sheeleigh School was named for Matthias Sheeleigh (1821–1900), pastor of the Lutheran congregations in Whitemarsh and Upper Dublin. The need for a new school resulted from the hiring of additional employees during the expansion of the Keasbey and Mattison Company. The Upper Dublin School District purchased a 200-by-225-foot lot on the corner of Argyle Avenue and Douglas Street for $1,250 from R. V. Mattison. Local builder Daniel Sperry got the contract for the building, which was to have four rooms on each floor, for $17,833. The cornerstone was laid in August 1906 and completion was in February 1907. When the school opened, there were four teachers, one of whom was also the principal. The building was torn down in 1969 because it was no longer adequate. A playground occupies the site today.

The Water Tower House was built near the Loch Alsh Reservoir in 1903 for the Ambler Spring Water Company, owned by Dr. Richard V. Mattison. The building, also known as the Doctor's Unique Tank House, was constructed to contain four apartments and five huge water storage tanks on the top floor. The tanks' capacity was 100,000 gallons. There are no stories of water disasters. However, the building was taken down in 1973.

Six

Fort Washington

Fort Hill was one of four hills on which fortifications were built in 1777. The fortifications were built during the Whitemarsh Encampment as a defense against the British advance after the Battle of Germantown. Fort Hill takes its name from the earthen redoubt built as a fort. This site is located in Fort Washington State Park.

Clifton House in Fort Washington was built on the site once occupied by Sandy Run Tavern. The Revolutionary-era tavern was named for the creek that flows nearby. Clifton House was used for quartermaster supply operations during the Whitemarsh Encampment of 1777. For 200 years, the building was in almost continuous use as a tavern, coach stop, and summer retreat for the well-to-do from Philadelphia. In 1936, the Historical Society of Fort Washington established its headquarters there. Maintained by the historical society, the building belongs to the state of Pennsylvania and is part of Fort Washington State Park. The historical society hosts monthly meetings on a variety of history-related topics. The reference library provides books and documents for researchers interested not only in history but also in genealogy.

Samuel Morris built the Union Schoolhouse along Bethlehem Pike in 1773. He was the first in the area to offer free public education for adults and children living within a one-and-one-half-mile walking distance. The contents of one original classroom from that school, including all furnishings and books and even the schoolmaster's hat, were moved to Clifton House. The museum is open to the public.

The Conard Auger Mill stood on Bethlehem Pike on the edge of the Sandy Run Creek. Built in 1714, the mill produced linseed oil until 1792, when it was sold to Albert Conard, who converted the mill to an auger-manufacturing plant. From 1905, when the property was sold, to 1919, it operated as the Montgomery Electric Light Company.

The smaller part of the house dates from the early 1690s and is believed to have been built as a hunting lodge by William Penn's physician and friend, Dr. Thomas Wynne. When Wynne decided it was too far to travel from his home, in what is now Wynnewood, he deeded the property to his nephew, who started what was possibly the first commercial venture in the area. He traded with the nearby Mondauk Indians for bear, wolf, fox, mink, and beaver fur. The next owner was Lord Petty, an Englishman who owned Petty's Island, in the Delaware River. He lost the property because of gambling debts. During the Whitemarsh Encampment, the house served as headquarters for Washington's surgeon general, Dr. J. Cochran. In 1969, Donald Gallagher, Esq., did extensive restoration to the house. Located on Pinetown Road, the home is listed on the National Register of Historic Places.

At the corner of Bethlehem Pike and Montgomery Avenue sits this farmhouse, built in 1759. While it maintains many original features including its springhouse, it is most notable as the home of Dr. Henry Elliger, for whom the area was later named Elliger Park.

The home at 215 Bethlehem Pike was known as the Half Way House when it served as the tollhouse on the Chestnut Hill-Spring House Turnpike. The stone above the third-floor window indicates the house was built in 1795 and bears the initials of Casper Schlater Jr., the county's treasurer and commissioner and a weaver by trade.

The first John Whitcomb in the area was born in 1751 and assassinated in Fitzwatertown in 1800. He had two sons. His son John was the first generation to be buried in the cemetery. He married Elizabeth Jenkins of Jenkinstown in 1810 and had seven children.

Located on Susquehanna Road, this small cemetery was the burial site of Whitcomb family members from 1803 until 1873. John and Elizabeth Jenkins's daughter Cyrene died when she was in her 20s, apparently before her parents. Her monument is large, with her parents buried on either side of her. Among others buried there are some Jenkins children and their families. One of the Jenkins's grandchildren was Matthew Fitzgerald Whitcomb.

In the mid-18th century, Philip Engard purchased 100 acres at the corner of Susquehanna Road and what is now Fort Washington Avenue. The house he built stands at the intersection. The area became known as Engardtown because of the many family members who resided here. Fort Washington Avenue was once known as Engardtown Road. Records from 1798 show a Jacob Engard at this location, but by the 1850 census, John Gamble was living at the property. Engard family members did own land and live farther from the intersection at this time.

This farm is on a six-acre tract on the northwest side of Fort Washington Avenue. The oldest part of the house dates from the mid-18th century, although there were significant later additions. Facing northwest on one of the outside walls is a beautiful Gothic window, left. It was a prototype for the Singing Towers of Mountain Lake Sanctuary in Lake Wales, Florida. Manufactured at the Enfield Pottery and Tile Manufacturing Company, the window is constructed of pastel green and blue tile, and depicts wildlife and plant growth. Since the late 18th century, the Gordon family has owned the farm, which is named Bopegan after three daughters—Bobby, Peggy, and Ann—who were born there.

The North Pennsylvania Railroad came to Upper Dublin in 1855. Less than a year later, on July 17, 1856, a horrific accident occurred at Camp Hill, resulting in 66 deaths. The original Fort Washington station was most likely wooden. Prior to train service to Philadelphia, Upper Dublin was an agricultural community with scattered farms, fields, woods, and streams. At first the train brought summer visitors to the area to enjoy the area's rustic beauty and cooler temperatures. By the 1870s, farmland was being purchased to build homes not only for summer visitors but also for residents who could travel to town by train. By 1895, the Reading Company sent 18 trains a day to Philadelphia. The present building is an improved structure erected near the beginning of the 20th century.

The Fort Washington Hotel opened in 1855 on the site of the earlier Wonderly's Inn. It was built to accommodate travelers at the end of the Fort Washington railroad line. It was home to the Fort Washington Lodge of the Masons from 1857 to 1868. The building looks much the same today as it did when constructed in Victorian times. At present, it houses a restaurant and provides rooms for people in the area.

The Sandy Run begins in neighboring Abington and runs through the southern portion of Upper Dublin. In the 1850s, it was noted for its trout and was stocked as early as 1895. Fishermen were fined $25 for using a net or fishing at night. As a result of 20th century development in the area, the stream has caused flooding in the Fort Washington area.

Many summer visitors, like the one pictured here, left the city of Philadelphia to enjoy the cool tranquility of the Fort Washington area. Although the train brought development, the area retained many natural places for recreation. The absence of heavy industry saved the area from the pollution that some developing places experienced.

Situated along Bethlehem Pike below Morris Road at Dungan's Field was a popular swimming hole for many generations of Upper Dubliners. According to the rule book, visitors could not throw stones, shoot, or destroy plant life or the property of others. A clock located in the gable of the house told all when it was time to leave. If one's watch did not agree with the clock, the watch was wrong.

Settled in the late 1600s, Upper Dublin was predominately farmland. Since this postcard was published at the beginning of the 20th century, it is difficult to know if this is a Colonial structure or a re-creation of one from earlier times. Records from 1798 indicate that 12 of 87 homes in the township were constructed of logs. Most of the other homes were made of stone.

This building along Bethlehem Pike just north of the railroad bridge stands relatively unchanged today. The Italianate design indicates that as early as the mid-19th century the area was changing from farmland to pockets of country homes. The building underwent a major restoration in the late 20th century and is now used for commercial purposes.

A post office was established in Fort Washington on December 9, 1878. The first postmaster was Abram Carn, who lived in this house on Bethlehem Pike. By 1907, the property also served as a drugstore. Upper Dublin had post offices at Gilkenson's Corner by 1827, Dreshertown by 1832, Fitzwatertown by 1853, and Three Tuns by 1854. The date of this post office indicates the area was growing and needing the service. At this time mail was not delivered to homes but was picked up at the post office. The building was torn down without warning in 2003 to expand a local auto dealership. From left to right are the following: (in front) Mary Schaffer (Huffnagle), Alice Carn, George Porter, and Ida Rediffer; (in the wagon) Albert Charles and John Craft; (on the porch) Abram Carn, Amanda Rediffer, and Alex Niblock, whose milk wagon is on the left.

Mechanic's Hall, officially the Junior Order of United American Mechanics, served as the center of community activities for many years. Built in the late 1800s, it was also known as Wissahickon Hall. It was used by social groups, for recreation, and for cultural events. The founding members of the Trinity Lutheran Church met in the hall before their church was complete.

St. Paul's United Church of Christ, at the corner of Morris Road and Bethlehem Pike, was formerly called St. Paul's Reformed Church. For many years the congregation was part of the Lutheran and Reformed Church of Whitemarsh, now known as Zion Lutheran Church, before separating and building St. Paul's in 1894. The edifice, constructed of gray and brown native stone, is an impressive Gothic structure of Liturgical style.

This *c.* 1910 view of Bethlehem Pike looks southward from the bridge over the railroad to Fort Washington. The building on the right is the Masonic Lodge (1868) and home to several stores. Some residents hoped that the trolley would bring business to the area while others objected to the lines passing their homes. Trolleys finally rolled up Bethlehem Pike in 1902.

Thomas P. Anshutz purchased the house at 212 Bethlehem Pike in 1899. The house and the barn date from the first half of the 18th century. Anshutz was a protégé of Philadelphia painter Thomas Eakins and succeeded him as dean of the Philadelphia Academy of Fine Arts. With Hugh Breckenridge, he opened a summer artist colony in Fort Washington, which brought talented artists each summer for the next 10 years. Anshutz died in this house in 1912 and is buried in St. Thomas Cemetery.

Hugh Breckenridge and Thomas Anshutz opened the Darby School of Art in 1900 in Fort Washington on Bethlehem Pike. Breckenridge's property at 208 Bethlehem Pike, known as Phloxdale, was built *c.* 1900 and was a centerpiece of horticulture. The large window on the upper story of the building was most likely used to enhance the light in the artist's studio. Breckenridge painted Woodrow Wilson's presidential portrait.

The Orchards was a home at 222 Bethlehem Pike, just across Ambler Road from the Anshutz colony. Bedrooms were added on the third floor to accommodate summer-school students. Since the majority of students were women, proper housing was important. Hugh Breckenridge and Thomas Anshutz grew apart as Breckenridge spent the summer of 1909 in Europe. Anshutz kept the school open without Breckenridge for the last two seasons before it closed.

This Bethlehem Pike accident scene, photographed on November 19, 1926, shows a portion of the artist colony just south of Ambler Road . The house on the left is the Anshutz home. The one on the right was moved from the site of the 1876 centennial celebration held in the Fairmount Park section of Philadelphia. Owner William Towne moved the building to this site, but it was a later owner, Edith Davis Seal Carpenter, who featured the house in "Furnishing the Little House," which appeared in the August 1926 issue of *Ladies Home Journal*.

This gracious house with its roof is located on the north side of Fort Washington Avenue at the corner of Susquehanna Road. The large wraparound porch and awnings, typical of 19th-century homes in the area, helped to keep the house cool. Constructed of local stone, the building has stood for more than 100 years.

This picture shows the 300 block of Fort Washington Avenue in 1912. Notice the dirt road sat lower than it does today. The majority of these homes still stand and remain relatively unchanged. The houses in the foreground are constructed of brick, an uncommon building material for the township.

By the beginning of the 20th century, Summit Avenue had changed from a summer vacation area to a year-round neighborhood. These stately Victorian houses on the 200 block show the middle-class neighborhood *c.* 1900. Many of these houses are still standing. The train station located at the end of Summit Avenue made this as convenient a location then as it is today.

Milton Bean built this house for the Reverend Mathias Sheeleigh in 1890. Bean was the same architect who redesigned the Mattison home in the Ambler area into a Scottish castle. Sheeleigh was an important person in the history of Zion Lutheran Church in Whitemarsh, Upper Dublin Lutheran Church, and Trinity Lutheran Church in Fort Washington. Although divided into apartments, the exterior of this structure maintains its basic design.

Built in 1888, this home on Summit Avenue reflects the change in the area from farmland to suburban neighborhood. The second-floor porch has been enclosed but the remaining structure is as it was when built. Like many houses in the neighborhood, it is built of local stone and wood. Located within a mile of this house, the quarry provided affordable building material.

The Trinity Lutheran congregation met at Wissahickon Hall on Bethlehem Pike as early as 1892. In 1897, the church was built on Summit and Spring Avenues, serving many of the families inhabiting the growing neighborhood of Fort Washington. Although families have moved away, some descendants of the original congregants attend church here to this day.

This double house was built in 1888 as a summer home for Philadelphia Ink manufacturer Charles Eneu Johnson. Designed by T. Frank Miller, the buildings originally included an ornamental barn, which burned in the 1950s. Pictured playing in front of the house are Bill and Bob Elton, whose family owned the house for nearly 30 years.

This Dutch Colonial home was built in 1895 for Ulysses Grant Funk. It was designed by Samuel Milligan of Philadelphia and built of locally quarried stone. Funk was one of the founders of the Fort Washington Fire Company. The Funk daughters served as local tax collectors for many years. The current owners are only the second family to live in the house.

Built in 1891, the Fort Washington School housed four classrooms until the larger school was built next to it in 1917. This early structure now serves as the gymnasium for the Montessori School that took over the building in 1969 when the new Fort Washington Elementary School was built. Removing the belfry and replacing windows with glass brick and modern sash significantly modified the exterior design.

Designed by Philadelphia architect Watson K. Phillips, the new larger Fort Washington School was opened in 1917. Its size describes the growth experienced in the area since the first school had been constructed. When this new school opened, most of its students lived in the neighborhood that stretched from Pennsylvania Avenue to Hartranft Avenue and from Fort Washington Avenue to Madison Avenue.

George Bodenstein was a prominent figure in the development of Fort Washington. A German immigrant, Bodenstein made his fortune as a chair manufacturer in Philadelphia. He built his mansion, Quellehof, in 1903 and contributed much to the community until his death in 1923. He is buried in St. Thomas Cemetery in Whitemarsh.

Pictured on the grounds of Quellehof are George Bodenstein with his wife, Elizabeth, right, and his sister-in-law Nellie Gossler. The Bodenstein mansion was large enough to house the numerous Bodenstein children, as well as Elizabeth's sister, who lived with the family because she was widowed.

George and Elizabeth Hartranft Bodenstein, far right, gather with their family outside Quellehof. They had seven children including George, Ellen, William, Paul, Helen, and Elizabeth. By the time this picture was taken, the eldest daughter, Ellen, was married to Samuel Craig and did not live with the family.

The Bodenstein family is pictured in the conservatory. From left to right are the following: (first row) Helen and Elizabeth Bodenstein; (second row) Paul, Elizabeth, and George Bodenstein, and Nellie Gossler (Elizabeth's sister). Judging by the clothing and the age of the girls, this photograph was likely taken in the 1920s.

Gazing out from the rustic gazebo are Esther and Naomi Gossler, great-nieces of George and Elizabeth Bodenstein.

The Bodensteins' youngest son, Paul, was a chemist. He may have worked at the nearby Keasbey and Mattison Company. By 1930, he had relocated to Petersburg, Virginia, where he was involved with the manufacture of artificial silk. At that time, he was married to a woman who had emigrated from Great Britain, and they had one daughter.

With the money George Bodenstein made in Philadelphia, he built this sprawling Georgian mansion on Madison Avenue. The Bodenstein estate covered many acres including a lake and a stream. He provided water to many homes in the village and was instrumental in the establishment of the Fort Washington Fire Company.

A doughnut-shaped lake was located at the rear of the property and provided a scenic spot for summer recreation for the family and invited guests. Natural springs below the Bodenstein property provided water for the mansion and the surrounding neighborhood. While the lake no longer exists, the springs are evident when the area experiences heavy rains.

The rear of the Bodenstein property had landscaped grounds that extended into the current office park. The juxtaposition of landscaped and natural areas was common to other mansions built near the end of the 19th century. This area has been developed and is now occupied by 20th-century houses.

Enjoying country life, Bodenstein family members take a carriage ride on a sunny day. Their style of clothing indicates this photograph was most likely taken in the first decade of the 20th century. Although automobiles were becoming more plentiful in the area, many preferred the more dependable transportation of horse and buggy.

The first floor of the Bodenstein mansion included a library. Adorned with handsome wood, the room has survived the many transformations that have affected the structure. The building was sold in 1946 and at some time became apartments. The current owners purchased the property in 2002 and are restoring elements of the mansion to their original elegance.

George Bodenstein acquired many properties in his Fort Washington neighborhood. This home, located at 231 Madison Avenue, north of the mansion, became the final home of his daughter Elizabeth, who died there in 1974. Elizabeth Bodenstein was the last of the immediate family to live in the Fort Washington area.

Monthly

Fort Washington 7/27/1903

The regular monthly meeting of the Fort Washington Heights Asso was held on above date the president in the Chair

No Minutes

The President named the following to serve on Committees

Road	Light	Finances
G Bodenstein	Wm Woorman	D. S. Grafly
John Burl	U G Funk	N. Dickey
Chas J Rogers	W R Arbuckle	F G Klosterman

The Treasurer Reported $10 — donation from Mr Kuemerly and a balance in hand of $53.82

It was moved and passed that Mr Burls bill for July lighting be paid $20.63

It was moved and passed to adjourn

WRA
Sec

As the year-round community became established in Fort Washington, a group of civic-minded men joined together to improve and maintain their neighborhood. Starting in 1903, the Fort Washington Heights Improvement Association met monthly and reviewed matters such as streets, lighting, and health issues. Among these men were representatives of the Bodenstein, Arbuckle, Ford, Sperry, Wallace, Conover, Dickey, Woorman, and Funk families. This picture is a copy of an actual page from the journal kept at the monthly meetings. The journal is preserved at Clifton House.

Founded in 1908, the Fort Washington Fire Company rented this garage or barn on Summit Avenue from George Bodenstein for its firehouse. The barn was used until a new firehouse was built in 1922 on the same land.

The Fort Washington Fire Company Ladies Auxiliary was formed in 1908. Many of the women served on a committee to support the fire company's first Labor Day parade and picnic. At the company's next official meeting following the parade, the firemen decided to form a permanent ladies auxiliary. The women are standing in front of a hose cart containing a watermelon bearing the words "Grown in Fort Washington."

The 1914 Pierce Arrow pumper stands in the front of the first firehouse. The Pierce Arrow chassis was purchased from George Bodenstein. After it was determined to be strong enough to be outfitted as a fire truck, Mr. Oberholtzer converted the truck in his wheelwright shop on Bethlehem Pike. The pumper was first put into action Christmas Day 1914 to assist at the Justice Lumber Yard fire in Glenside.

In 1928, the Fort Washington Fire Company purchased a Seddon chemical fire truck from the company located in Flourtown. This was the only one of its kind built there. Fire company fund-raising events like oyster dinners and flea markets are as much a part of the community as the fire company itself.

Members of the Fort Washington Fire Company No. 1 pose in front of a fire truck prior to participating in a parade in 1953. They are, from left to right, as follows: (first row) George Haggar (assistant chief), Charles Wiley, George Painter, Russ Maxwell, Harold Davies (assistant chief), Walter Coombs (assistant chief), and Dominic Mallozzi (chief); (second row) Bud Robert, Charles Teller, Howard Baily, John Foley, Walter Neithercott, Marlin Miller, and Harold Nathan; (third row) Bob Wiley, Don Jacobs, Harry Teller, Ralph Wright, Howard Cooper, and Bob Wenzel. Depending on volunteers since its inception, the company has protected the community from fire for almost 100 years. These residents serve in the proud tradition of those who served before them. A second station opened on Susquehanna Road in 1976 to meet the needs of a growing township.

In 1955, ground was broken across the street from the earlier firehouse for the third Fort Washington Fire Company firehouse. Dedicated in 1956, the building serves the community to this day. The old firehouse was sold to become a dentist's office.

Homes are visible in the 200 block of Summit and Madison Avenues, and the 1956 firehouse is in the foreground. Today, this part of Fort Washington is much the same as it appears in the photograph, which, judging by the automobiles, was probably taken in the 1960s.

A July 1963 fire claimed Old Main, on the Ambler campus of Temple University. Here, Fort Washington firefighters assess the damage and declare the structure a total loss. It was not until 1970 that a full-time fire marshal was hired. The development of the industrial park increased the need for expanding the fire company.

The stable complex and clock tower are a small part of the Camp Hill Hall estate in Fort Washington. The estate was built in 1882 by John R. Fell for his bride, Sarah Drexel. The mansion had 43 luxurious rooms. After her husband's death in 1895, Sarah Fell married Alexander Van Renssalaer and continued to enjoy Camp Hill. After the Van Renssalaers died, Fort Washington Military Academy was located at the estate for a few years. In 1951, the Worldwide Evangelization Crusade took over Camp Hill.

Fairwold, on Pennsylvania Avenue and Camp Hill Road, was built for Philadelphia banker Craig Heberton. Heberton hired Wilson Eyre Jr. to design the house for him and his wife. Richard and Emily Cadwalader purchased the home after their marriage in 1909 and added the ballroom in 1923. Following his wife's death, Cadwalader sold the home to his real estate agent, George Gay. After living in the mansion for a few years, the Gay family gifted part of the property to the Oreland Baptist Church. Gay's will mandated that the building always be used for religious purposes. It now houses a Reconstructionist Jewish congregation and the Play and Learn Center.

This grand entrance was intended to impress visitors to Fairwold. Furnished with artwork and rich fabrics, it indicates a time when the wealthy spared no expense in decorating their homes. This photograph was part of a brochure that Freeman's Auction produced when the Cadwaladers sold the estate in 1941.

The Cadwaladers decorated their living room in High Revival style. The heavy furniture and plush textiles help to warm this immense room. Since the Cadwaladers maintained a residence in the city as their primary home, this room most likely saw entertaining during the summer months. It is, nonetheless, decorated in a fashion of which high society would approve.

The two chandeliers and placement of pier mirrors brightened the French Provincial–style room. The Cadwaladers were enormously rich, socially prominent Philadelphians, who entertained often in their summer residence. The light-colored walls and mirrors served to brighten the sometimes dark interior of the mansion.

Richard and Emily Cadwalader added this ballroom in 1923. Designed by DeArmond, Ashmead, and Bickley, it was rumored that the roof was retractable when the ballroom was first built. However, the original plans do not support the retractable-roof theory. This wing of the mansion now serves as the home of the synagogue Or Hadash.

The Oreland Baptist Church modified the ballroom of Fairwold in 1949 for use as their church, which was founded under the leadership of the Reverend Herman W. Heppe. The church began by initiating residential home gatherings throughout the small settlement of Oreland in October 1893, when Heppe was still a theology student. A chapel was built on a lot donated by the Orlando Land and Improvement Company and located at the corner of Orlando and Rech Avenues. On June 30, 1894, the first meeting was held in the new chapel. The congregation had outgrown the chapel when George B. Gay offered the use of a large portion of his estate. Dedication services were held on April 3, 1949. The church disbanded in 1987 and sold its portion of the building to New Life Presbyterian Church. The building was taken over by Or Hadash in June 1995.

The first major road in the township was Limekiln Pike (1693). Other early roads included Welsh Road (1712), Bethlehem Pike (1714), Jenkintown Road (1725), Butler Pike (1739), and Norristown Road (1751). This picture, from the beginning of the 20th century, was most likely one of these roads. The lack of paving indicates the rural nature of the township at this time.

Warren Self, right, delivered oil, installed oil-heating systems, and founded Self Oil Company in 1946, after World War II. Early in 1960, his son Robert Self introduced air-conditioning service, and since then, the business has been known as Self Heating and Cooling.

The Self Farm began in the 1920s with a one-room house. The family raised and sold corn and vegetables on the 28-acre farm. Farming continued until 1955, but it was not until 1995 that land was sold for a housing development.

Frederick Sloane Arnold built this Victorian house in 1902 at 1305 Fort Washington Avenue. He started a butcher shop and slaughtered animals, some of which he raised himself. He became a huckster and maintained a small grocery store. The property remained in the family until the late 1990s.

After many years as a huckster, Frederick Sloane Arnold was prosperous enough to purchase a truck. Pictured with the truck are, from left to right, Charles Santee Arnold, Frederick Sloane Arnold, and Virginia May Arnold.

Now a barbershop, this unimposing structure was the sales office for the Elliger Park development. In 1925, Potts Brothers began constructing suburban homes on land once owned by Dr. Henry Elliger. For many years the family has continued to build houses in the area, and owners take pride in identifying their homes as "Potts-built."

This aerial view of early Elliger Park was produced by Potts Brothers to help sell the homes the company planned to build. Bethlehem Pike runs from right to left at the bottom of the picture. The roads running from the top to bottom of the picture, starting at the right, are Fort Washington Avenue, Washington Lane, and Elliger Avenue. Notice that there are many homes on the right side of Fort Washington Avenue and that the land in Elliger Park is mostly uncleared. On the left, structures along Bethlehem Pike can be seen. The first home in the community was completed in 1925. At the time Potts Brothers was building, the style of architecture that was popular was Colonial Revival. Many homes in Elliger Park reflect this style. Building continued in Elliger Park for the next few decades, and today, the area remains a desirable neighborhood.

In 1901, the Hoopes and Townsend Iron and Steel Company moved from Buttonwood Street in Philadelphia to an area that is now occupied by an office park. The company relocated in part because of its proximity to two railroad lines: the Reading spur and the Trenton cutoff of the Pennsylvania Railroad. The company hit the height of its production during World War I. The village of Hoopeston grew up around the factory, providing homes and a store for the workers. Due to the swampy conditions, at least five children died each year in Hoopeston, and the smoky haze from the plant ruined the air quality. The factory closed in 1925 and was demolished in 1928. In the 1950s, the land became home to a 600-acre industrial park. As industry left the area, buildings were converted into office space, and many large office buildings were added.

Like many company towns, Hoopeston had a company store. In these stores, workers spent their wages and the company earned more money. Rental housing was built for employees along Pinetown Road and Highland Avenue to further connect the workers to the company.

By the mid-20th century, the company store had become a restaurant. The Coach Inn building, shown in this 1963 photograph, was where local residents enjoyed fine dining. The addition of railroad cars was very popular with diners. Currently, a restaurant serving South Asian food and a Subway sandwich shop occupy the building.

The area of Highland Avenue below Pinetown Road has changed little since this photograph was taken. The new Fort Washington post office was constructed in the late 1990s. The road to the right that once led to Hoopeston now serves as an entrance to the office park.

This Sunoco station was located on Bethlehem Pike, south of the railroad bridge in Fort Washington. From 1932 to 1937, it was owned by Jim Warren and his father, Samuel Warren, a retired Philadelphia mounted policeman. In addition to gasoline, oil, minor repairs, oil changes, and lubrications, customers could buy sodas and snacks. Outside grease pits served as the Jiffy Lube of their day. Although the roofed forecourt is gone, the building behind it still stands and has been used for several businesses. Due to bridge improvement and the temporary closing of Bethlehem Pike, the most recent business has closed and the future of the structure is in question.

ACKNOWLEDGMENTS

The Historical Society of Fort Washington is indebted to many people for assistance in publishing this book with Arcadia Publishing. It would not have been possible without the hard work of the book committee: William Amey, Sylvia Holteen, Lewis and Trudy Keen, Ingrid and Tom Rivel, and Robin Costa.

We are grateful to the many community members and institutions who gave us information and allowed us to include their photographs in the book. In addition to the photographs in the collection of the Historical Society of Fort Washington, images were shared by Joanne Alberger, Ambler Church of the Brethren, the *Ambler Gazette*, Fred Arnold, Milton and Marybeth Barba, Tom and Claire Barlow, Libby Boggs, Arlene Bowes, Gus and Jenny Carey, John Costa, Robin Costa, Jim and Dena Dannenberg, John E. Davey, John and Elsie Detweiler, Fort Washington Fire Company No. 1, Ted and Martha Gay, William Gordon, George Haggar, Bob Hibbert, Robert Holmes, Sylvia and Ned Holteen, Margo Irwin, Jarrettown United Methodist Church, Nick Jennings, Mary Lou MacFarland, Dr. and Mrs. Paul Mailshanker, Montgomery County Historical Society, Newt Howard Collection, Old York Road Historical Society, Ken Potts, Queen of Peace Roman Catholic Church, Questers' Salt Cellar-Chapter 329, Betty Roberts, George Schmallenberger, Frederick Schmidt, Chuck and Carol Schramek, Mary Seiriano-Winslow, Sharon Shapowal, Carol Shaw, Springfield Township Historical Society, Dorothy Sutton, Temple University Archives, Jim and Nan Warren, Al Whitcomb, and Sandra Wilson.

In addition to using the resources of the Fort Washington Historical Society's library, we benefited from the assistance many others provided by researching and compiling information about the community. We would like to thank Joan Cressman Avera, Bill Gift, Nick Guilbert, Miriam Gay James, Tom and Carol McGlumphy, Dick Meyer, William Paxson, Phoebe Rosenberry, David Rowland, Elizabeth Saddler, Sally Spiwak, Eileen Troxell, the late Evelyn Wright, and Edward Zwicker.

A project of this magnitude could not have happened without the help of numerous people, and the potential of omitting someone is possible. We hope no one was overlooked.

www.ingramcontent.com/pod-product-compliance
Lightning Source LLC
LaVergne TN
LVHW081542100826
845153LV00004B/291

* 9 7 8 1 5 3 1 6 2 0 4 3 1 *